Mix and Mash

Written by Hatty Skinner

Collins

Tip the cups in.

Mix the wet things.

Tap the shell.

Tip it in.

Chop and mash them.

Mix it.

Put them into tins.

Fill them.

Tip on choc chips.

Put the tins in.

Ping! Quick! Get the muffins.

Yum!

/v/

14

 After reading

Letters and Sounds: Phase 3

Word count: 40

Focus phonemes: /w/ /x/ /y/ /qu/ /ch/ /sh/ /th/ /ng/

Common exception words: and, into, the, put

Curriculum links: Physical development; Understanding the world

Early learning goals: Reading: read and understand simple sentences; use phonic knowledge to decode regular words and read them aloud accurately; read some common irregular words

Developing fluency

- Your child may enjoy hearing you read the book.
- Take turns to read a double page, encouraging your child to pause at the end of each sentence. Check they read **Ping!**, **Quick!** and **Yum!** on pages 12 and 13 with extra emphasis.

Phonic practice

- Ask your child to sound out and blend these words:

  ch/o/p   w/e/t   th/i/ng/s   m/a/sh   m/u/ff/i/n/s

- Turn to page 12 and point to **quick**. Ask your child to read the word and find the two pairs of letters that each make one sound. (*qu/i/ck*)
- Look at the "I spy sounds" pages (14 and 15) together. Point to and sound out the /v/ and /w/. Say:I spy a /v/ in "vegetables" and point to the vegetables. Encourage your child to do the same, finding /v/ things in the picture. (*volcano, violin, vase, vinegar*)
- Point to the /w/ and say: I spy words that begin with /w/ like "whale". (Point to the whale.) I can see things with /w/ in the middle and end too, can you? Help your child find words containing /w/. (*window, sunflowers, whisk, bow, waffle*)

Extending vocabulary

- Reread page 4, then point to **tap**. Ask your child: Which of these could we use instead of **tap** – crack, drop or pick? (*crack*)
- Reread page 6, then point to **mash**. Ask your child: Which of these could we use instead of **mash** – tip, squash or cut? (*squash*)
- Can your child think of another word for **mix** on page 7? (*stir*)